Ocean Limits

Contents | Page

written by Rachel Walker

Planet Earth is different to all the other planets we know about because it supports human life. The reason Earth can support human life is because it has oceans. These huge seas are our life support system. Oceans supply the people of the planet with the food we eat, the air we breathe, and the water that we use. Without oceans people could not exist.

Oceans work like a giant filter, keeping the Earth habitable by driving the natural forces of Air, Water and Weather, which maintain life on our planet.

- The rolling sea creates more than half of our planet's oxygen supplies.
- More than 97% of Earth's water is ocean, so we need oceans to feed the water cycle and supply our fresh water.
- Oceans drive Earth's weather systems too – producing air currents and affecting temperatures.

A healthy ocean means more than clean coasts and thriving ocean wildlife. The health of the oceans directly impacts the health of the people around the world. If the ocean isn't healthy, neither are we. Healthy oceans are essential.

Impacts

For thousands of years, human activity has had serious impacts on the natural forces governing our planet. In the last 100 years, and in particular the last 50 years, those impacts have been massively destructive. So it's vital that people must now defend the health of our oceans – i.e. stop causing damage to them and protect them against:

- global warming
- pollution
- negative fishing practices.

To protect our oceans, communities need to make sure that human activities are sustainable: this means that they must meet the human needs of present and future generations **without causing any more harm to the environment.**

Unsustainable fishing is
the biggest single threat
to our oceans. Over 70%
of fisheries are already
exploited to the limit of
what is sustainable, or
beyond. Larger fish are
being wiped out, so the next
smaller fish species are
targeted, and so on.
We must save our oceans
and sea life for the long-
term health of the oceans
and the people of the world.
Governments can impose
tougher limits on catches
and then patrol their zones
to make sure that the
fishing fleets:

- stick to their quotas and
  don't overfish
- don't fish in protected
  areas.

Commercial over-fishing = oceans in crisis

Scientists are warning us that modern industrial over-fishing methods have already done massive damage to the world's oceans, which may never recover. Now people are competing for even less fish as commercial fishing fleets, using sonar technology, can target schools of fish quickly and easily.

Around the world, fishing is big business. Billions of dollars are made in the fishing industry, supporting over 200 million people by providing them with jobs and wages. They want commercial fishing to continue so new sustainable fishing technology is being developed that will radically change the global fishing industry for the better. In time, the new "Precision Seafood Harvesting" technology will replace traditional trawl nets. The break-through design of the harvesting system allows fishing vessels to target specific species and sizes. This greatly increases protection both for small fish that can swim free through "escape portals", and for unwanted species, which are released unharmed.

Bycatch is one of the most serious environmental impacts of commercial fisheries. Because different kinds of fish live together in complex ecosystems, fisheries often catch fish other than the one species that they are targeting. When this happens, these unwanted fish are just thrown dead or dying back into the sea. Latest reports suggest that at least 8% of the total global catch is wasted. Every year, fishing nets kill up to 300,000 marine mammals such as small whales, dolphins and porpoises. Thousands of sea birds and sea turtles are killed each year too, as a result of becoming entangled in fishing nets.

Some fishing practices destroy habitat as well as sea life. Bottom trawling, for example, destroys sensitive habitats like coral reefs and can harm other delicate ecosystems as the sea bed is ripped up. When these habitats are destroyed, it can make it difficult for sea life to feed, breed and hide from predators.

trawl net

Global warming effects

Scientists say that warmer ocean temperatures will raise sea levels and even change ocean currents. Whole species of marine animals and fish are at risk due to the temperature rise – they simply cannot survive in the changed conditions. For example, increased water temperatures are thought to be responsible for ice forming later in the year and lasting for fewer months. Polar bears need the ice floes to live on and to hunt from.

Another major impact of human activity on the health and wellbeing of the world's oceans is pollution. We treat the sea like a giant waste disposer or toilet, by allowing the dumping of:
- domestic and farm sewage
- toxic discharges such as chemicals from factories
- urban and industrial waste
- oil tanker leaks
- mining run-off
- agricultural nutrients and pesticides
- dangerous radioactive discharges.

TOXIC

Communities need to change the way that the people of the world think of the oceans, and how they treat them, because the way we all manage the ocean and its resources will have an impact on everyone, too. First we have to know that we have serious problems, and then we have to take action to change the future. People need to protect the oceans and the creatures that live in them, so that the oceans can continue to be our life support system:

- making our oxygen
- feeding our water cycle
- providing essential food
- supplying minerals vital for our health and survival.

Our survival depends on the health of our oceans!

Positive change

One thing that will have a massive positive impact on the health of the oceans is if more and more marine reserves are created in big areas of the oceans. Marine reserves are zones where the oceans are protected from human threats like fishing and pollution. At present less than 1% of the world's oceans are protected, compared to 12% of the land.

If just 10% of the world's ocean area was set aside as marine reserves, then the oceans would have a much better chance of healing, and the world's future would be secure. If this happens soon there is a chance for the oceans to repair themselves and become healthy again.